GUINNESS
BOOK OF
ASTOUNDING
FEATS & EVENTS

**BY NORRIS McWHIRTER
& ROSS McWHIRTER**

Illustrated by Kenneth Laager

RL 6, IL 5-up

GUINNESS BOOK OF ASTOUNDING FEATS & EVENTS
*A Bantam Book / published by arrangement with
Sterling Publishing Co.*

PRINTING HISTORY
Sterling edition published July 1975
Bantam edition / November 1975
2nd printing . . . December 1974
3rd printing . . . July 1976
4th printing . . . June 1977
5th printing . . . May 1979

All rights reserved.
Copyright © 1975 by Sterling Publishing Co., Inc.

Based on the Guinness Book of World Records
*Revised American Edition © 1974, 1973, 1972, 1971, 1970,
1969, 1968, 1966, 1965, 1964, 1963, 1962
by Sterling Publishing Co., Inc.
© 1960 by Guinness Superlatives Ltd.*

*This book may not be reproduced in whole or in part, by
mimeograph or any other means, without permission.
For information address: Sterling Publishing Co.
419 Park Avenue South, New York, N.Y. 10016.*

ISBN 0-553-13070-6

Published simultaneously in the United States and Canada

*Bantam Books are published by Bantam Books, Inc. Its trade-
mark, consisting of the words "Bantam Books" and the por-
trayal of a bantam, is Registered in U.S. Patent and Trademark
Office and in other countries. Marca Registrada. Bantam
Books, Inc., 666 Fifth Avenue, New York, New York 10019.*

PRINTED IN THE UNITED STATES OF AMERICA

0 9 8 7 6

INTRODUCTION

Facts and feats can be more astounding than fiction and fantasy. After 20 years of combing the world for the most astounding feats and events for the GUINNESS BOOK OF WORLD RECORDS, we realize that some of the feats included in this book seem unbelievable.

We want to assure our readers, however, that every feat and event illustrated is true and accurate. You can believe every statement made, for we have checked and authenticated everything.

NORRIS McWHIRTER and ROSS McWHIRTER

"The Human Cannonball," Emanuel Zacchini, got shot 175 feet in the air at a speed of 54 miles per hour at every performance of the Barnum & Bailey Circus for many years. It was the record distance for firing a human from a cannon, but often his daughter, Florinda, got shot out with him. Eventually, she took over the job, and the management was fortunate in finding that she was a girl of the same caliber.

"Mr. Bubble" from Sterling, Colorado, is the top bucking bull of the rodeo world. He weighs 1700 lbs. and is called No. 17. When cowboys do manage to ride on his back, they win first place in any contest.

Allan Stewart finally dislodged his opponent, Joe Oliver, after 3 hours 15 minutes in the longest log rolling contest on record. This was in Ashland, Wisconsin, in 1900, and the log was 24 inches in diameter.

The world's heaviest polar bear, weighing 2,210 lbs., was shot in 1960 while he was guarding the entrance to a bay in Alaska. When mounted for display at the Seattle World's Fair, he measured 11 feet $1\frac{1}{2}$ inches tall. The average polar bear weighs 850–900 lbs. and is $7\frac{3}{4}$ feet long.

Face slapping is a popular sport in Russia and some parts of Scandinavia. The men keep at it until one calls a halt or is knocked over. The longest contest on record in Kiev, Russia, in 1931, was declared a draw after 30 hours. This record was beaten in 1974 in the Odd Ball Olympics in Los Angeles when Bruce Stewart and Robert Argust kept it up for 31 hours.

Without a parachute, Lt. I. M. Chisov of Russia had to bail out of a damaged plane from 21,980 feet up in 1942. He lived to tell the tale, and set a record for the longest fall without a parachute, because he fell on the steep side of a snow-covered mountain and slid to the bottom. He broke his pelvis and damaged his spine, but recovered.

Lying on a bed of needle-sharp nails 6 inches long for 25 hours 20 minutes is the record held by Vernon E. Craig, also known as Komar. At one time he held a golf cart on his chest while on the bed of nails, and another time he held 4 men standing on a board weighing a total of 1,142 lbs.

"Simba," an 11-year-old black-maned lion, is the heaviest member of the cat family. He weighs 826 lbs. and lives in the Colchester Zoo in England.

No one has ever exceeded the record of 11.0 seconds set in April 24, 1909, for 100 yards running three-legged. It happened in Brooklyn, New York, and the runners were Harry L. Hillman and Lawson Robertson.

The shortest full-grown woman who ever lived was 23.2 inches high at her tallest. Called "Princess Pauline," she was 12 inches tall when she was born in Holland in 1876. At the age of 4 she was only 15 inches tall and at 9 she was 21.65 inches and weighed only 3 lbs. 5 oz. Her mature weight varied between 7½ and 9 lbs. She died when 19 years old of pneumonia.

The man who has been king of a country longer than anyone else living is **King Sobhuza II of Swaziland**, Africa, who has reigned since he was 5 months old in 1899. His country was placed under the protection of Great Britain when he was born, and given its independence when he was **69 years old in 1968**. The all-time record holder was Pharaoh Pepi II of ancient Egypt who reigned for **91 years**.

In one of the most gruesome disasters of all time, a man-eating tigress ate 436 human beings in India before being shot by Col. Jim Corbett in 1907. The only episode of this kind which could approach this was when 1,500 people in Kenya were killed by a group of 22 man-eating lions in 1941—42, before 18 of them were shot.

The first heavyweight title boxing match with gloves lasted 21 rounds of 3 minutes each. "Gentleman Jim" Corbett (left) won over John L. Sullivan in the bout which took place in September, 1892. Corbett held the title until March, 1897, when he was knocked out by Bob Fitzsimmons, the lightest heavyweight champ (167 lbs.) to wear the crown.

How high and far can a horse jump? "Huasó," ridden by Capt. A. L. Morales of Chile set the official high jump record at 8 feet $1\frac{1}{4}$ inches in 1949 at Santiago. The longest jump recorded was 27 feet $2\frac{3}{4}$ inches over water by "Amado Mio" in Barcelona, Spain, in 1951. There is a claim that a horse named "Heatherbloom" cleared 8 feet 3 inches and covered 37 feet in 1903, but this was not officially verified.

The largest car ever produced for road use was the Bugatti "Royale," known as the "Golden Bugatti." Only six were made in France by the Italian designer, Ettore Bugatti, starting in 1927. The car measures 22 feet in length, the hood is over 7 feet long, and the 8-cylinder engine has a 12.7-liter capacity. Some of the six cars are still in existence. A longer car was custom built by Duesenberg for Greta Garbo in blood red in 1933. It measured 24 feet overall.

Many paintings are priceless, but the highest price ever paid for a painting in a public auction was $5,544,000 for this picture by Velázquez, the Spanish artist, in 1970, after being owned by the family of the Earl of Radner of England for many years. It is a portrait of Velázquez' slave, painted as an "exercise" in 1649 by the painter before he attempted a portrait of the Pope.

The longest opera regularly performed is Wagner's "Die Meistersinger" which lasts 5 hours 15 minutes. A still longer opera, "The Life and Times of Joseph Stalin," which requires 13 hours 25 minutes for its seven acts, has been performed only four times.

Taller than the Statue of Liberty is this statue called "Motherland" in Volgograd, Russia. Standing on top of a hill, it measures 270 feet from its base to the tip of the sword. It was designed in 1967 to commemorate the Battle of Stalingrad during World War II.

The biggest invasion in history was the Allied invasion of Normandy, France, lasting 3 days beginning on June 6, 1944. It included 745 ships and 4,066 landing craft, carrying 185,000 men and 20,000 vehicles, as well as 1,087 airplanes carrying 18,000 paratroopers with an air cover of 13,175 other planes.

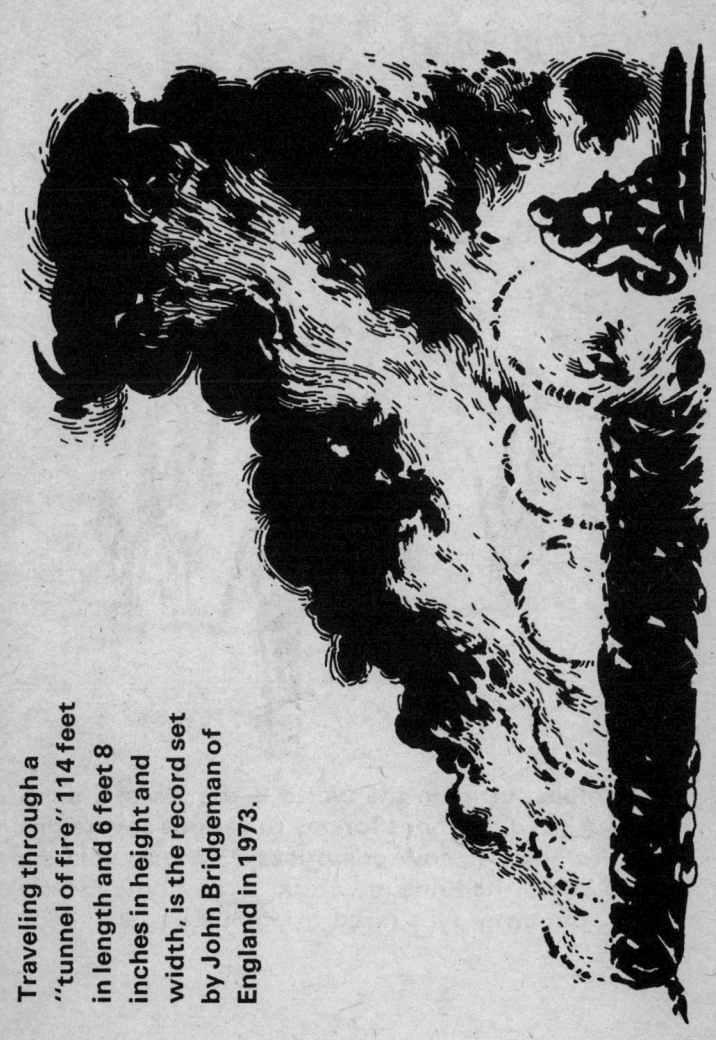

Traveling through a "tunnel of fire" 114 feet in length and 6 feet 8 inches in height and width, is the record set by John Bridgeman of England in 1973.

The oldest army in the world is the Swiss Guard,
which hired itself out for pay to various sovereigns
before 1400. It now comprises 83 Swiss soldiers
who guard the Pope in Vatican City, Rome, where
the army was hired originally in 1506.

While blindfolded, Frank Keith of Naperville, Illinois, wrote legibly upside down, backwards and inverted in mirror fashion. It was the only case of its kind ever reported. Although Leonardo da Vinci, the famous Italian artist, wrote everything mirror fashion, he did this with his eyes open.

Kenneth LeBel set a long jump record over barrels on ice skates when he leaped over 17 of them, a distance of 28 feet 8 inches at Liberty, New York, in 1965.

A team of 12 boys from a school in Swindon, England, pushed a hospital bed through the streets for 724 miles in 1973.

Chris Redford of England once (in 1973) put 39 coins on his forearm near his elbow, flipped his arm forward and caught all the coins in the same hand. It set a world record for coin snatching.

How long can a moustache grow? The answer is 102 inches, as a Brahmin Indian named Masuriya Din, born in 1908, proved in measurements made between 1949 and 1962. The upkeep cost him $30 per year.

Staying perfectly motionless for $4\frac{1}{2}$ hours is the record set by William Fuqua of Fort Worth, Texas, who gets $1,300 per hour working as a fashion mannequin. One time he got stabbed by a man who wanted to prove to his wife that Fuqua was really a dummy. After three weeks in the hospital, Fuqua improved his security to prevent others from pinching, poking, pouring water on him or undressing him while at work.

The greatest miser of all time was undoubtedly Hetty Green, who died in 1916, leaving an estate of $95 million. Yet she lived in poverty, eating mostly *cold* oatmeal because she was too stingy to pay for gas to heat it. Her son had to have his leg amputated because she spent too much time trying to get *free* medical service. She died of a stroke while arguing that skimmed milk was as good as whole milk.

In filling a fountain of champagne glasses 16 high from the top, Jean Jouas, a sommelier at the Pont Neuf restaurant in New York, set a record on the David Frost–Guinness TV show in October, 1974.

The record for meat eating was set in 1880, when one whole roast ox was eaten in 42 days by one man, Johann Ketzler of Munich, Germany.

No one has ever beaten the record of keeping 44 plates spinning at the same time while atop poles about 5 feet high. The feat was accomplished by Holley Gray of England on a British TV show in May, 1970.

Dancing the Charleston for the longest time without a stop—25 hours—was the record set by Tom Garrett, 23, in Pensacola, Florida, in 1971.

The record for jumping over a billiard table hasn't been broken since 1892, when Joe Darby of England cleared the 12-foot length of a table starting from a 4-inch-high solid wooden block.

The shortest war lasted 38 minutes. Admiral Rawson of the U.K. battle fleet gave Zanzibar's Sultan an ultimatum, then bombarded the island until he surrendered.

Snail eating is an art, and Rex Miller of Texas (shown here) is the style champion. But a woman named Mrs. Nicky Bove of Houston won the record for eating 124 snails in 15 minutes.

The longest ride in full armor was 146 miles by
Dick Brown, 42, in 3 days 3 hours 40 minutes in
June, 1973. He rode from Glasgow to Dumfries,
Scotland.

When it comes to crawling with at least one knee always on the ground, Aubrey Dodd of Wanganui, New Zealand, is the world record holder. Crawling 6.46 miles in 6 hours, making 26 laps around a 440-yard track, is the record he set in 1974.

The joke telling record is held by Ken Dodd who told jokes unremittingly to paying audiences at the Royal Court Theatre, London, for 3 hours 6 minutes on June 4, 1974.

Staying under a shower bath for a record 175 hours 7 minutes was the feat achieved by David Foreman of Niagara University in 1973. The record for females is 98 hours 1 minute by two girls, Paula Glenn, 18, and Margaret Nelson, 20, in Britain in 1971.

In official pie-throwing contests held in England, the target face must be 8 feet $3\frac{7}{8}$ inches from the thrower and the pie no more than $10\frac{3}{4}$ inches in diameter. Six points are scored for a square hit full in the face. A championship contest is held in England every year.

A man who has spent many years collecting different brands of cigarettes is Dr. Robert E. Kaufman of New York. At last count he had 6,612 different brands from 163 countries in his cigarette library, the oldest being "Lone Jack" from about 1885.

In attempting suicide, Sarah Ann Henley failed when she jumped from the Clifton suspension bridge in England in 1885, but she set a world record for the longest fall—250 feet. What saved her life were her skirt and petticoat which acted as a parachute. She landed in the mud with just bruises.

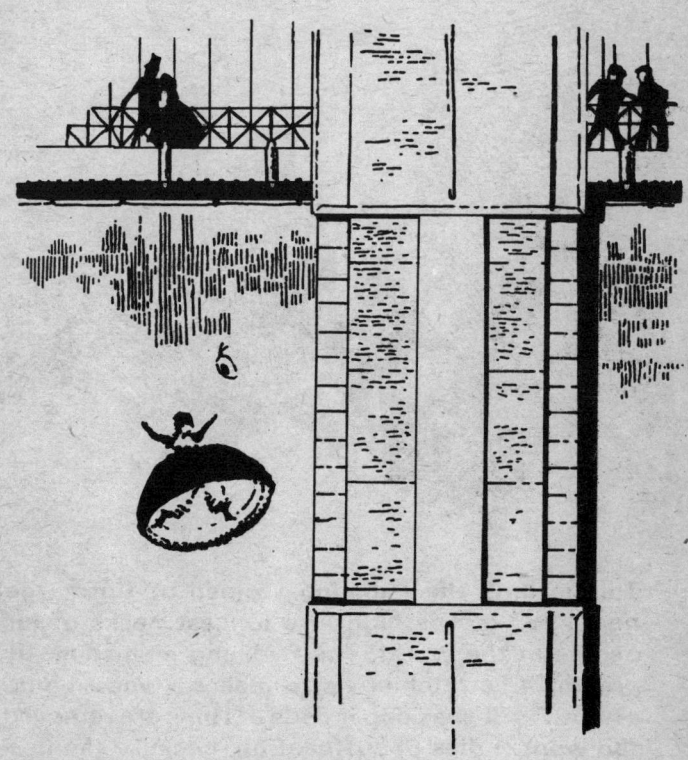

This is how the Padaung women of Burma get necks 15¾ inches high, the longest necks of any people in the world. The Padaung men think the practice of stretching necks makes a woman more attractive. If the copper coils or rings are removed, the woman dies of suffocation, because the neck muscles have gotten so weak.

For 133 days (4½ months) Poon Lim of Hong Kong survived alone on a raft after his ship was torpedoed 565 miles from land in the Atlantic in 1942. He was rescued by a Brazilian fishing boat.

On her first trip in 1909, the world's largest con-
verted icebreaker, the "S.S. Manhattan," 1,007
feet long and 150,000 tons, made the first double
voyage through the Northwest Passage of the
Arctic Ocean, northern Canada to Alaska and back.

The largest non-rigid airship ever flown was this Navy ZPG 3-W, which had 1,516,300 cubic feet capacity, was 403.4 feet long, 85.1 feet in diameter and had a crew of 21. First flown in July, 1958, it crashed into the sea in June, 1960.

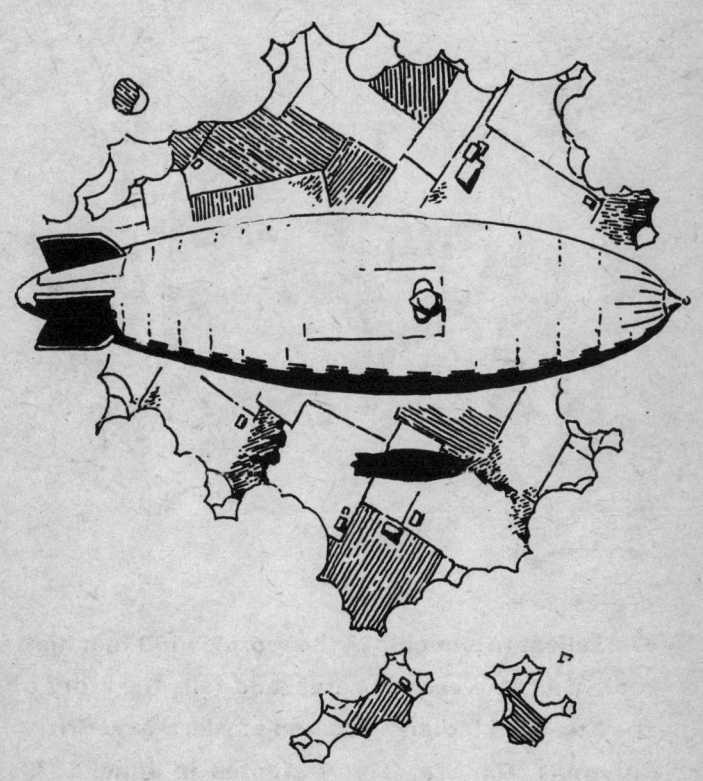

The tallest totem pole in the world is 173 feet high, took 36 man-weeks to carve, and tells the story of the Kwakiutl Indians. Located at Alert Bay, British Columbia, Canada, it was erected in June, 1973.

How far can a man throw a standard 5-lb. brick? Robert Gardner threw one 142 feet 6 inches in a 1971 contest in Gloucestershire, England.

How fast can a helicopter fly? The world's fastest whirlybird is the Sikorsky S-67 Blackhawk which set a record of 220.885 m.p.h. in December, 1970, when it was flown from Milford to Branford, Connecticut, by a test pilot. A helicopter boosted by turbojet engines can go 316.1 m.p.h., an unofficial speed record set in 1969.

The longest beard known was worn by Hans Langseth of Norway, who died in 1927. It was an incredible 17½ feet long. If you want to see it, it has been preserved in the Smithsonian Institution in Washington, D.C.

The greatest battle of World War II and the greatest conflict of armored vehicles ever was the Battle of Kursk in July, 1943, on the Eastern Front, when 3,600 Russian tanks repelled a German Army with 2,700 tanks. Some 1,300,000 Red Army troops with 20,000 guns and 3,130 aircraft backed up the tanks.

Napoleon as Emperor of France left his mark in history at many places. Even his hat, last worn by him in 1815, set a world record for the highest price ever paid for a chapeau—$29,471.

The greatest explosion of modern times occurred when Krakatoa, an Indonesian island of 18 square miles, erupted and killed 36,380 people, wiping out 163 villages. Rocks were thrown up 34 miles and dust fell 10 days later 3,313 miles away. The explosion has been estimated to have had about 26 times the force of the greatest H-bomb detonation.

The oldest astronomical observatory still standing is this structure, called Chomsongdae, built in 632 A.D. in Kyongju, South Korea.

The largest cigar on record is this English monster, 5 feet 4½ inches long and 10½ inches around at its widest point. It was made by a London company and is housed at the Northumbrian University Air Squadron in England. Other claims of larger cigars have been made but not verified.

The world's longest bus is 76 feet long and seats 121 passengers. Although it is manufactured in Indiana, it is in use only in the Middle East.

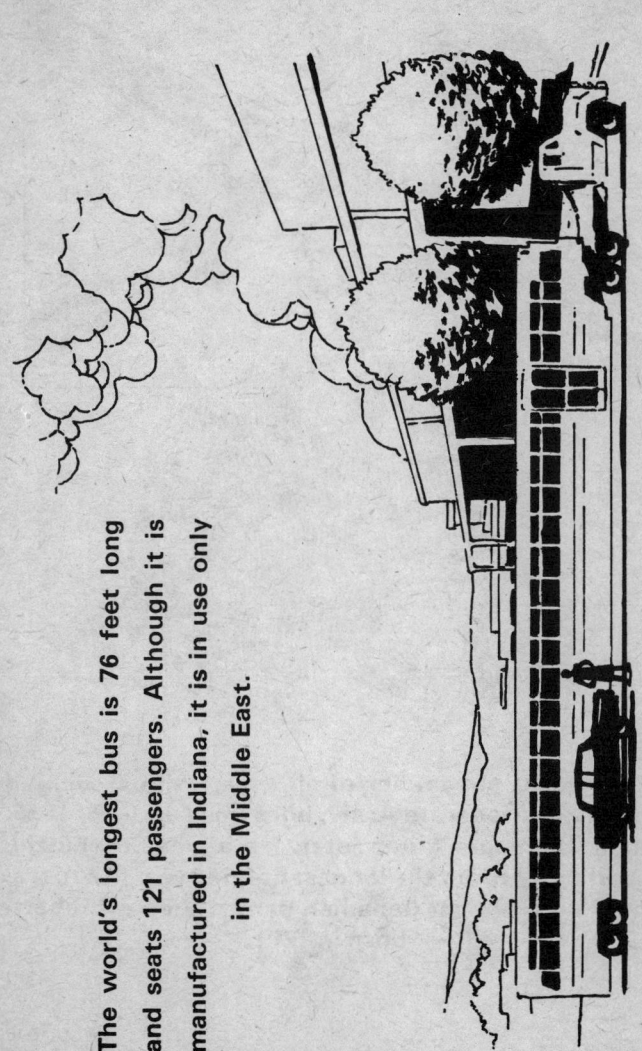

The oldest old soldier of all time, John B. Salling of the Confederate Army, born on March 15, 1846, died 113 years 1 day later. He almost broke the world record for the longest life, 113 years 124 days, held by a French Canadian named Pierre Joubert, born in 1701.

Ice yachting is not a sport for everyone, but attaining a record speed of 143 m.p.h. in a stiff wind can make it exciting. This ice yacht, the "Icicle," was built for Commodore John E. Roosevelt in about 1870 and raced on the Hudson River. With 1,070 square feet of canvas, it was the largest ice yacht ever built.

Not a coin for one's pocket was the Swedish copper 10 daler of 1659, which weighed up to $43\frac{1}{2}$ lbs. It set a record for the heaviest metallic coin.

Not the highest but the largest cable cars in the world operate at Squaw Valley, California. Built in Switzerland, they can carry 121 persons on the 7,000-foot-long cable.

The largest rope ever made was 47 inches around, and was used in 1858 to launch the British liner, "Great Eastern," then the largest ship of its time at 18,914 gross tons.

Water for New York City comes through the longest tunnel of any kind in the world—85 miles from the Rondout Reservoir in the Catskill Mountains to Hillview Reservoir in The Bronx. The tunnel is 13½ feet in diameter and was completed in 1945.

The car speed record in 1907 was a remarkable 150 m.p.h. set by Fred C. Marriott in his Stanley Steamer at Ormond Beach, Florida. Steam-driven cars may be on the way back, as they use no gas, and are propelled by a turbine.

The longest telephone call on record lasted for 724 hours when a fraternity at Morehead State University in Kentucky was connected by phone to a sorority at the same school in January-February, 1974. Students took turns talking.

Sit in a tree 12 feet up for more than 56 days? That is what Norman L. Zellers of Mattoon, Illinois, did at age 13 in 1930. Why? Just because there was a cottonwood tree in the front yard.

For 3 hours the Rev. Henry Whithead talked, delivering the longest after-dinner speech on record. This occurred in 1874 in the Rainbow Tavern, London. Today in England, there is a Guild of Professional Toastmasters whose founder, Ivor Spencer, has listened to 25,000 speeches. It has only 12 members and elects the most boring speaker it has heard each year.

The oldest newspaper still in existence is a Swedish official journal first published in 1644, by the Royal Swedish Academy of Letters. The "most smoked" newspaper is the "South Pacific Post," published in New Guinea. Its circulation is only 5,200 but paper is so scarce in the area that after it's read it's used for cigarette paper, although now another newspaper is competing and the paper shortage is eased.

Parking meters were invented by an American named Carl C. Magee and were first installed in the business district of Oklahoma City on July 19, 1935. They were an immediate success.

"Snowshoe" Thompson is the man responsible for introducing skiing to America from Norway in 1856. Skiing thus began in California about 27 years before it started in the Alps, where it was not introduced until 1883. The first ski club was founded in 1861 in Australia. Ski racing did not start officially until 1911, when a downhill race was staged at Montana, Switzerland.

The smallest colony in the world today is Pitcairn Island in the South Pacific near Tahiti. It is British, founded by Fletcher Christian and other men who mutinied against Captain Bligh of the "Bounty" and had to flee with the ship. Today the island of $1\frac{1}{2}$ square miles has 82 inhabitants.

The longest voyage recorded for a message in a bottle is about 25,000 miles. The bottle was dropped on May 27, 1947, in the Pacific, and picked up on the shore of the island of Sylt in the North Sea, off the coast of Germany, on December 3, 1968.

You would expect people in a cold country to drink more coffee than any other—and you would be right. The world champion nation for coffee drinkers is Finland, where 37.30 lbs. of coffee were consumed by the average person in a year in 1970.

No convict ever escaped from the world's most secure prison—Alcatraz—during the time it was used, 1934–62. On an island in San Francisco Bay, Alcatraz recorded 23 escape attempts. One man reached the mainland alive only to be recaptured on the spot. The rest were either drowned (6), shot dead (5) or recaptured (11).

An event of shocking impact was the explosion in Halifax, Nova Scotia, in 1917 when a lucky man named William Becker was blown 1600 yards (almost a mile) out of town and found still alive, in a tree. In the explosion, 1,963 people were killed, and some say the death toll was 3,000 because many bodies couldn't be found.

These holed stone discs, called Fé, are the coins used in the Yap Islands of the Western Pacific, the most massive coins in the world. One medium-sized coin (as shown) is worth one Yapese wife or an 18-foot canoe. The biggest are 12 feet in diameter, and weigh up to 185 lbs.

The poorest people in the world are the Tasaday tribe of cave dwellers in the Philippines, who were "discovered" in 1971, living without clothes, domestic animals, agriculture, pottery or wheels. It's too soon to tell if they will be happy about being discovered.

The largest pearl ever discovered weighs 14 lbs. 1 oz. and is 9½ inches high by 5½ inches in diameter. Found in 1934 in a giant clam in the Philippines, it was worth $4,080,000 in 1971, is owned by Wilburn Dowell Cobb, who keeps it in a bank vault in San Francisco. Called the "Pearl of Lao-tze," it is rough, a baroque type.

The heaviest bell in the world is within the Kremlin walls in Moscow. Cast in 1733, it weighs 216 tons, is over 19 feet high, 22 feet 8 inches in diameter, and 24 inches at its thickest point. It is cracked, and a 12-ton fragment is broken away.

Who has the heaviest brain? No, it's not the smartest man—it's the sperm whale. The brain of a 49-foot-long male whale weighed 20.24 lbs. when it was extracted aboard a Japanese factory ship in 1949, compared to 15.38 lbs. for a larger blue whale, and 16.5 lbs. for a big elephant.

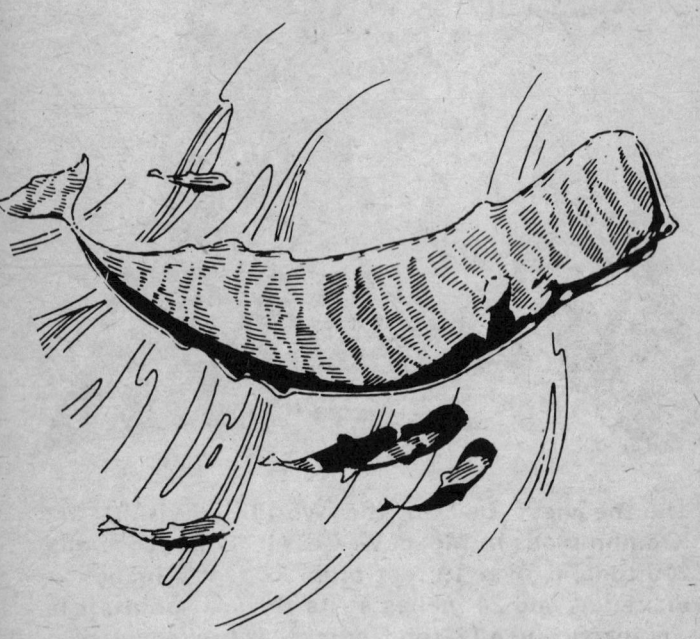

The most massive castle ever built was this chateau in the Department of Aisne, France, which had walls 22$\frac{1}{2}$ feet thick. Built in the 13th century, and standing 177 feet high, it was leveled by the Germans in 1917.

You can almost depend on "Old Faithful" erupting every 66 minutes. This geyser in Yellowstone National Park, Wyoming, sends its spire of steam and water 140 feet up in the air, and it has only missed its schedule by 21 minutes in all the years it has been recorded.

Before recorded history—about 75 million years ago—in Montana and Wyoming, this dinosaur roamed and lived by devouring smaller animals. Known as the Tyrannosaurus, it was the largest of the predatory creatures, 47 feet long and $18\frac{1}{2}$ feet tall, and weighed 8 tons.

A hailstone weighing 1.67 lbs., measuring 7½ inches across and 17½ inches in diameter fell in Coffeyville, Kansas, in 1970, to set a world record for hailstones. They form in the clouds when raindrops freeze and collect together, then are released during a thunderstorm.

Skid marks 6 miles long? Yes, it happened when Craig Breedlove was trying to set a land speed record in 1964 and his car, the "Spirit of America," went out of control on the Bonneville Salt Flats in Utah.

Greenland, with about 840,000 square miles, is the world's largest island. (Australia is more than 3 times as large, but it is generally considered a continent.) Some experts say that Greenland is really several islands overlaid by an ice-cap, but the ice never melts enough to be sure.

The oldest national flag in the world is that of Denmark. Red with a white cross, it was first carried in 1219 in the Battle of Lindanissa in Estonia.

Fjords in Norway extend inland quite a distance from the sea as the Vikings discovered. The longest fjord which is not an arm of a ''sound'' is Sogne Fjord, which extends 113.7 miles inland and is barely 3 miles wide.

The world champion cowboy is Larry Mahan, born in 1943, who won 6 world titles between 1966 and 1973. He set a record for prize money—$64,447— in 1973, in contests for bareback bronco riding, calf roping, bull riding, saddle bronco riding, and steer wrestling, the events of the rodeo.

To test wood-cutting skill, 12-inch logs of Australian hardwoods are placed in standing blocks. Record holder C. Stewart chopped through the log in 13.7 seconds in 1965.

Hoop rolling can be fun—but rolling a hoop 600 miles in 18 days?! That is exactly what Zolilio Diaz of Spain did in 1968. He went from the town of Mieres in northern Spain to the capital, Madrid, in central Spain, and back.

Lobster tales are almost as plentiful as fish tales. The largest lobster that didn't get away measured 3 feet from the end of its tail to the tip of its claw and weighed 42 lbs. 7 oz. It was caught off the Virginia coast in 1934 by a trawling fishing smack and is now on exhibit in the Museum of Science, Boston.